FINISHING LINE PRESS

www.finishinglinepress.com

The Darks and the Lights

poems by

Sarah Stoltzfus Allen

Finishing Line Press
Georgetown, Kentucky

The Darks and the Lights

ACKNOWLEDGMENTS

"Beacon Hands" was originally printed in the June 2021 issue of *Sparked Literary Magazine*

There are so many people to thank for helping me on the road to making this happen, but I'll keep this short and sweet. Thank you, Silas and Elijah, for providing the necessary distractions (and noise) that led to many of these poems taking weeks (possibly years) to finish. Thank you for being you. You have changed my entire life for the good and everything you are makes me want to be better. I hope you know that I always try and that we can do hard things. Mom and Dad, I wouldn't be here without you. Take that in every way you can imagine. Phyllis Swartz, what would I do without you pointing out my need for a hyphen in my compound adjectives? Thank you for always taking the time. Thank you to the rest of the Bethel Camp Writer's Network for reading my words and helping me scribble. It means the world! And to the person who doesn't want to be thanked, thank you from the bottom of my heart. You make life better.

Publisher: Leah Huete de Maines
Editor: Christen Kincaid
Cover Art: Kristin Kremer
Author Photo: Rebecca A. Stoltzfus
Cover Design: Elizabeth Maines McCleavy

Order online: www.finishinglinepress.com
also available on amazon.com

Author inquiries and mail orders:
Finishing Line Press
PO Box 1626
Georgetown, Kentucky 40324
USA

Table of Contents

To the sons of my heart and blood and tears,
you can do hard things.

Bedtime Stories

He'd curl her close and hold her tight
and let the words dance in the air.
The dragons soared and knights did fight,
he'd curl her close and hold her tight.
She'd gasp and laugh, her mind take flight,
he'd breathe new worlds for his girl fair.
He'd curl her close and hold her tight
and let the words dance in the air.

His whiskered face would brush her cheek
as steadfast hands tucked her in snug,
his warm brown eyes her blues would seek,
his whiskered face would brush her cheek.
Before those words of love did speak
he'd ask for one more final hug.
His whiskered face would brush her cheek
as steadfast hands tucked her in snug.

"Guess what!" He'd smile and whisper near,
and then she'd grin and close her eyes,
"I love you!" on the air appeared.
(Guess what he'd smile and whisper near.)
The two would say the words with cheer
like each had won a special prize.
"Guess what!" He'd smile and whisper near,
and then she'd grin and close her eyes.

Songs from the Mountain Top

The sun burns away night mists,
cleaning the sheen of restless sleep
from my face and limbs.

*

Hold me in your arms,
precious trees.
Whisper me your truth,
reveal the lies that breed
disease in my leaves and roots.

*

You have never failed me—
the sun warming long-sleeping wildflowers,
and dew crystals shimmer
whenever I am with you.

Once I crest the ridge,
inhale the clean air,
you are mine
and I am yours.

*

Hours pass in your golden green—
chittering squirrels,
fluttering sparrows,
and even a lazy garter snake
sunning himself three rocks over.

They know I belong here with them
and it's been far too long
since we have seen each other.

*

The redbuds have bloomed
and finally I can breathe.

Breathe.

Dust Rag

You are the white of years-washed
soft cotton, stained daily
with machine oil, dirt, and sweat—
the smell of outdoors man,
red-skinned from the elbow down,
back-breaking work
that kept beans and cornbread
and fried potatoes in the bellies
of all those gifts from God.

Bleach, and Granny's stain-removing
secrets, could only do so much
before your home became the bucket
under the sink
instead of the bottom drawer
of Papaw's antique dresser.

Cornbread

I've tried, at least, one hundred different cornbread recipes.
One hundred different suggestions
on cornmeal, cornmeal mix, self-rising flour.
One hundred different ingredient measurements and ratios.
Add baking powder and more salt.
One recipe even called for cornstarch.

I've used sheet pans,
and when that, obviously, failed
I relieved my mom's kitchen cabinets of
pyrex dishes, cake pans, and
cast iron skillets.

Really, there was no failure.
Each one tasted good.
I mean, you slather anything with enough butter
and it's going to be delightful.

But...

it wasn't *her* cornbread.

It wasn't my Granny's.
It didn't taste like an apron
that had dried my tears,
or soft, childbearing hips that would scoot
me out of the way
so I didn't get burned.

It didn't taste like how her face
scrunched up when she laughed
or how, no matter what we did,
my hair always got caught in her glasses
when she hugged me.

It didn't taste like sitting at her dinner table
and sneaking a bite
while the love of her life said grace.

My cornbread didn't taste like home.

After a year-long pursuit
of perfect cornbread,
I can proudly say I've found it:

2 cups buttermilk corn meal mix
2 large eggs
2 tablespoons melted bacon grease
1 3/4 cup buttermilk

Preheat your oven to 400 degrees.
Turn your stove on to medium high heat,
put a huge spoonful of bacon grease in a cast iron skillet
and let it get screaming hot on the stove
while you whisk all the ingredients together.

When your skillet is sufficiently hot,
pour your batter into the skillet,
remember what granny's house smelled like
and put it in the oven for 25—30 minutes.
Whisper memories of granny's kitchen
into the warm air of your own
so they seep into the wooden spoons and
measuring cups and mixing bowls.

When the cornbread is a deep golden brown,
remove from the oven and turn it out
onto your prettiest plate.
While it's still steaming,
spread salted butter all over the top.
Inhale your heritage.
Cut a piece and savor all those cooks before you.

Share the rest with the people you love most.

Now, after a year of making some of the
best cornbread my husband
(a self-proclaimed northerner)
has ever put in his mouth, I can proudly say

my cornbread still doesn't taste like home.

But, if I'm lucky,
my cornbread will taste like home
for someone else.

Beacon Hands

They laid you on my chest,
all pink skin and wrecking wails,
and I knew what I should feel,
what I should say and do.
Even waking from sedation
I knew my face should beam and glow.
There should be joyful streams of tears,
and bonds snapping into place.

Instead, an icy numbness
crept across my pubic mound
where they pulled you from my body,
and I imagined the doctor
had stitched a glacier in your place—
the only logical thought I had
in those first few desperate days.

Once I dreaded to admit
that all I felt when you were born
was frigid blackness.
Fear, world-cracking fear,
had snaked its frosted fingers
up my spine and ribs and throat
till I was frozen,
made all of arctic water, bitter snow;

but if I don't admit that,
admit that utter bleakness,
what reason could there be
to tell the world of beacon hands
swirling above my heart
where you latched onto my breast?

What reason to tell how you blazed
for months and months,
shining light in all my darkest places,
exposing every fear and anxious thought
as something to face and recognize,
own, then burn away in your brilliant flame?

Not admitting my darkness
means dimming the spark turned wildfire.
Fire breeds fire and you
consumed everything in your path
for better and grace and all things
patient on this good earth.

You made me want to live.

I still feel the tip of the glacier
poke my abdomen from time to time,
still feel frost begin to creep
into my bones and settle in my belly;
but you seem to burn the brightest then.

You feel the cold sneaking in.
You see it in my face.
You hear it in my words.
You swirl your beacon hands,
pushing warmth and light into my winter—
until I see the blaze
that leads me home.

Growing Memories

Today, we held hands
and breaths
as we tip toed into clear,
cold mountain water.
I watched as you carefully
let go of my hand,
then charged knee deep,
perpendicular to the current;
watched as you lost your footing
on the loose, silty creek bed.
I reached out my hands to you,
but you did not reach for me.
Independent and drenched,
you found your own way to the bank
of that frigid mountain stream.
I made note of your autonomy
and closed my fingers
around a gentle breeze.

Later, dry and eating sandwiches,
I lay back on the scratchy grass
and closed my eyes,
felt you beside me,
even though you made no sound.
You put your shoulder to my shoulder
and your head to my head.
I opened my eyes and turned;
your almost three-year-old eyes
smiled into mine.
A toothy grin broke across your face
and your nose brushed mine.
I made note of your dependence
and closed my arms around you.

All of you.

Chocolate Smudges

I will always think of you
with chocolate smudges
on your smile and
brilliant face,
sneaking pieces into pockets
and warm hands.

While I want to stop you
(for the laundry's sake),
I never do;
I just pretreat the stains
and never let you
wear white.

One day you will
concern yourself with
napkins and appearances,
but until then
I'll breathe in chocolate
every time I ask
for a kiss.

Dear Storm Crow,

Do you plan
the disturbances?
Or do they sprout organically
from your brilliant mind?
Do you, as they say,
wing it?

I won't say there was peace
before you came
into your own,
but there was
predictability.

But you,
I am not afraid to admit,
have made Mischief
a proper noun.
It is the fifth person
in our four-person
family.

I wonder, often,
what travels through your mind
at the speed of light.
What incites your body
to move
while the rest of us are content
in stillness?

What tectonic shift goads
your mouth to speak?

I guess they don't really matter:
the inciting instances or tectonic shifts
or the unpredictability.
You are you, Storm Crow,
Son of my blood and tears
and marrow.

If you always speak
in riddles,
I will love you
no less.

Dirty Laundry

You are grass-stained knees
and ketchup drips on church pants,
primary colored paint splashes on
school uniforms and socks that smell
like only little boy feet can smell,

red wine on a favorite blouse,
amorous stains on bed sheets,
sweat and motor oil soaked into
t-shirt cotton,
the good towels that have cleaned up
pirate bath time adventures.

You are dirt and love and tears,
blood and water mixing,
flowing into all things new.

Traveling

Yellow lights zooming
through dark, rain-slick
windows stained with the
graven images of grief.
I'm convinced that the face
I see reflected back to me
will stay this way:

a ghost traveling beside you.

The glory of new life
still shining in your eyes,
you don't see me wince
at the mention of grand adventures

and then hide behind
gallant gestures
of blinking away tears
and smiles
and "absolutely!"

Through the smudged night,
I see myself as this gothic woman.
Never seen, but
gilded in forever melancholy,
a mystery even to those who love her,
who will smear on red lipstick
to make a brave face.

I will drive these Georgia highways,
as long as you like,
as long as it is dark,
as long as the music keeps you singing.

And pray that the grace given to you,
will someday extend to me.

Penelope

Sometimes I let the words
curl down my arms until they
seep into the
darkness with you.

And sometimes
I prick my finger for this endeavor
so that words swirl and stain
into some semblance of order.

But most often
I let the words come as they will
without fight or fear
because the page
that tear-stained
long-suffering friend
listens best.

Hello, Morning

You are still dark—
quiet and sleepy
night webs cling to
the corners of my eyes
and wrap me in silent shawls
I'm terrified of tearing.

Shall we huddle
over warm drinks and the
leftover playfield of
last night's adventures?

Did we know each other
prior to that first little boy?
Did I ever seek out your still comfort,
your solid presence?

No matter, now.
You, dear friend keep me
grounded.

Secret keeper.
Dream reminder.
Courage finder.
Tear Collector.

That's who you are.

We gather in the stillness,
pray together,
clean up forgotten trains,
and you remind me

why the sun comes up.

Stained

I imagine myself
a white coffee cup,
the kind found in good diners.

I fit hands well
and hold heat for the longest
possible time,
letting tired fingers
curl around me and take
what is needed:
warmth and
energy and
slight addiction.

I wear the marks
of dregs left too long
over conversation and
someone else's lipstick.

Harsh cleaning
has chipped my pristine glaze,

the imperfections
would not wash away
no matter how hot the water.

To All the Men Who Have Claimed to Love Me

I pass a funeral home,
every morning,
on my way to work.
Most days I drive
and see nothing—
no activity,
no death.
It seems just another
house on the Main Street
of my every day.

This time there were three stretchers
lined up outside the side entrance.

I have no idea who
lost their lives,
who will no longer
open eyes to blue skies;
any kind of sky for that matter.

I just know three people
are dead.

But this is not a murder poem.

I have no intention of
wishing death,
or even suffering, on you.

I see your wives
your babies and
your perfect little lives.
I won't lie;
I play the what if game
regularly.

But I don't want you.

Or anything you have.

Even if you took pieces of me
that left me helpless
and vile and
less than whole.

Because I know
I'll never be whole
and I've stopped trying
to get those pieces back.

So today I imagine
myself in three body bags
lined up outside
a funeral home side entrance
awaiting a mortician.

And I allow them
the chance to wash you away,
exonerate my skin of
every cell of you.

Because Lord knows
I've tried purging you
from every corner of
my splintering rib cage.
Tried scrubbing you from
the laugh lines and crows feet
and the memory of
hands on my hips.

But it never works.

This isn't a reborn poem either.

So today
I put to death the me
I was with you.

Here's hoping
she stays
dead.

Indelible

I want to write my name
alongside yours
in every visitor's book,
at every opportunity—

old churches, local exhibits,
country inns where we
slipped beneath floral duvets
and whispered love and lust—

take the pen from your
hand, smile when you fit
your palm into the small of my back,
and ink myself into
history with you.

The Darks and the Lights

You can find hundreds of dreamy,
romanticized poems
about the men in my life:
my love, my dad, my boys.

But not a single one about the person
who actually keeps me together.
The person who, without fail,
makes sure that I am living.

There is no way to romanticize
cleaning up after me
or changing the sheets
when I've been sick
and didn't make it to the bathroom.

Nothing dreamy about keeping me
in clean clothes and doing dishes
and going to doctor's appointments
(where she still holds my hand).

How do you write a poem
about learning to separate
the darks from the lights
or how to measure flour the correct way
or how she believed me when no one else did,
holding me, her grown child, to her chest
in the middle of the night
when I couldn't tell the difference
between dreams and the cool darkness
of my childhood bed?

I can't make any of this ethereal.
It's not pretty.

It is hard work and real.
It's learning to be long-suffering and dependable.
It's all the things in life that really matter.

My dad? He taught me to read,
to sing from my belly,
and to dream.

My mother, who continues to give me life,
taught me how to make those
dreams come true.

Being with You

Being with you is
the start of a green, curved path.
I don't know the end,
but holding your hand, walking
unknown places, is enough.

Love Poem

Every poem is a love poem.

I've written hundreds of them already
so what else is left to say?

Only this:

Sons of my heart and blood and tears,
when I have to make the choice,

I will always choose you.

Sarah Stoltzfus Allen, above all else, loves a Terry's dark chocolate orange on Christmas morning. She's a mom, an avid earl grey tea drinker, and she tolerates her cat. When she gets the time, and sometimes she has to make it, she writes poems, hikes the hills of her beloved Eastern Kentucky home, and dreams outlandish dreams. What seems like a lifetime ago, she studied music education and creative writing at Morehead State University. You can find her published in various online and print journals and if you catch her not looking, you could sneak a peek at her journal. She lives, and loves, in her small house on the edge of a hill in West Liberty, Kentucky and can't imagine life anywhere else.